D0814013

THE NATIONAL POETRY SERIES was established in 1978
to ensure the publication of five poetry books
annually through five participating publishers.
Publication is funded by the Lannan Foundation;
Stephen Graham; Joyce & Seward Johnson Foundation;
Juliet Lea Hillman Simonds; The Poetry Foundation;
Olafur Olafsson, Mr. & Mrs. Michael Newhouse;
Jennifer Rubell; The New York Community Trust;
Elizabeth Christopherson; and Aristides Georgantas.

———— 2011 Competition Winners ————

The Apothecary's Heir
by Julianne Buchsbaum of Lawrence, KS
Chosen by Lucie Brock-Broido

Your Invitation to a Modest Breakfast
by Hannah Gamble of Chicago, IL
Chosen by Bernadette Mayer

Green Is for World
by Juliana Leslie of Santa Cruz, CA
Chosen by Ange Mlinko

Exit, Civilian
by Idra Novey of Brooklyn, NY
Chosen by Patricia Smith

Maybe the Saddest Thing
by Marcus Wicker of Ann Arbor, MI
Chosen by D. A. Powell

Green Is
for World

POEMS

JULIANA LESLIE

COFFEE HOUSE PRESS
Minneapolis
2012

COFFEE HOUSE PRESS books are available to the trade through our primary distributor, Consortium Book Sales & Distribution, cbsd.com or (800) 283-3572. For personal orders, catalogs, or other information, write to: info@coffeehousepress.org. Coffee House Press is a nonprofit literary publishing house. Support from private foundations, corporate giving programs, government programs, and generous individuals helps make the publication of our books possible. We gratefully acknowledge their support in detail in the back of this book. To you and our many readers around the world, we send our thanks for your continuing support.

Good books are brewing at coffeehousepress.org

LIBRARY OF CONGRESS CIP INFORMATION

Leslie, Juliana.
Green is for world : poetry / by Juliana Leslie.
p. cm.
ISBN 978-1-56689-316-9 (alk. paper)
I. Title.
PS3612.E77G74 2012
811'.6—DC23
2011046606

FIRST EDITION | FIRST PRINTING

1 3 5 7 9 8 6 4 2

PRINTED IN THE U.S.A.

ACKNOWLEDGMENTS

THANK YOU to the editors of the following journals, where some poems first appeared: *Omni-Verse, Perihelion,* the *Poetry Loft,* and *West Branch Wired.* "That Obscure Coincidence of Feeling" first appeared as a chapbook for *Dusie Kollektiv* 3 (2009).

In the poem, "The Age of Parts," the line "a footnote to Ovid's radiance" is adapted from Norman O. Brown's essay, "Metamorphosis III: The Divine Narcissus." In the poem, "Margaret Fuller," some words and ideas are adapted from Margaret Fuller's writings.

Thank you to Eric Baus, Peter Gizzi, Noah Eli Gordon, Sawako Nakayasu, and Joshua Marie Wilkinson for continued friendship and support. Thank you to Ange Mlinko for selecting this book for the National Poetry Series.

for Michael Labenz and for Cosmo

Dream Canary

Welcome to the hard edges
the curvier tough
of geranium lengths and tubes
a world figurative in prim
the beginning of earth
its equivalent arrow
or something
masters of evening in hats
like rocks

Bernadette

What's more
as in bed
I consider the details   the sequins
the singular plural of being the kids
in the street
and everything I learned
who personifies joy
in democratic sheets
who belongs on the verge
in parentheses   briefly
and to others

If this is what it takes
to groom a phrase from trees
when the end and the middle meet
in the electrons
See the pith we finesse
the guts everyone eats
a breath at the end of reading
an image gets stuck
in our collection our leggings
of expansion

Poem with Moveable Parts

We rode the crowded bucket
over bumps
it was not terrible
in history's head
a big thing is here
somewhere
democracy sends its flowers
into space
and space waits
to be covered gently
by paper
There are women who wear
external forms of hope
on their collars
there is
the newly emergent
like a crush
a perfect piece
of air
how we dive into vessels
with our hands
how we bury
the whole eight and three-thirds
of a mossy thought
in the middle
It was not ineffable

these voices
sometimes they get lost
and picked up again
like Odysseus in his fifteenth year
even Odysseus can be
a sunny taste
on a sensitive page
We'll have to finish this later

My Name Is Helen

This is my moment
my shirt unbuttoned
my own drift
in the dreamstory
of the unhappy pope
myself on the lawn unbuttoned
in the displeasure of the dream
announcing
the self divides twenty-eight thousand
in fours and fives
and the pears blink;

*

My life at the edge
of a different kind of line
if you were the right kind of person
Our nature is more natural
Our self-improvement is hungry
dreaming in Spanish
turning oneself over in one's own mind
turning yourself over
in another's hand
with an eyelash

to the wheel
or planting a little garden
with tomatoes either way;

*

You were dutifully recorded in a book
you studied hard and read Shakespeare
you said
having written several hundred pages in a daybook
learning to be a better man
when other men
were driving cars
through sand;

*

If California is a planet
if *I* is a swamp
the pleasure of this voice announcing
Clear and low clouds
leading us toward
asking
how young is too young
to invent the angle

of the name you live in
to erase the edge of the margin
and master the subject of painting;

*

I want you to have
these works on paper
these pieces of paper
falling from the sky
Each piece falling according
especially the sums
in dramatic space
these elementary conditions
paper plus air
plus volume;

*

What kind of body would require
an unprecedented need
for friendship
to be the beloved
of someone's love
and quest for detail

down a dirt path
in the middle of nowhere
as thinking is to undressing;

*

The fair new is everyone
who talks about
what you can see under
illuminated pressures
Southern exposure is a charm
New England blinks after shipwreck
"I died in a shipwreck"
she said
the ship blinks

Something about Bundles

This is what you do
with a list
let the air in

Mercury doesn't freeze
it flashes

Life doesn't
let the grassy
box open without

The Dress I Wrote Backward

She slipped into time's knot curled up
She slept in her arms false or true
She dynamic twin palms
trims the stubborn trees
unpleats sun from sharp edges
moving backward in a dress
one by one between
a figure to think a figurine
She was troubled by many
naming them elements carbon or pulse
She sent balloons into the great
the blue-headed year
and being economical
pairs together in frames the triple
one block of ticking as she
the parallel expert of night
cuts her own hands
how prosody swallows
before you go
joining simple laws to the wind
She what relates to a graph
is omnipresent maximal
coming to a standstill in wood
She heavy traffic having driven
around the end of the edge of
the pursuit of formal steam

She glimpses artists of the moment
painting the pelvis the ulna the remnants
the red gestures in single moments that bend
in the innermost of schools
the combinations figure themselves
as in epics or symphonic sheets
She watching from the inside
what utopia loves in utopia
milk in her hair
and ankles

Late Life

Can we be appearances
in cafés
remixing hope?
I approach my arms
at the bank   as in line
I update my failure
I run the hem you pitch to me

I'm starting to understand
how to measure
by which I mean
the right-handed in July
leaves his voice
in the grass

The Obtuse

At first everything is poised
A spongy man unfolds himself
It's as if we lived in the late baroque
as if under a sign of plenty
or an actor's waxy dance

If a reader's role is to think or sell
a mirror image a left-handed rose a figure eight
What if the reader
is a lemon? What if earth
weighs less?

The Implied Reader

If anyone knows something
about anything
life's flexible
carnations
the endlessly flexible sense
of tomorrow
opens and the story ends
when the sun
flips

That Obscure Coincidence of Feeling

Charm the pants off
dearly beloved
we are passing through
A driver unsure he is a part of himself
is pressed into his private arms
A morning in trousers
contains volumes
His hubcaps
announce the difference
Her ankles
are artichokes

*

Lumps in the reading
produce diplomacy as if
when the weather
is full of people
like powdered sugar
My desire is to argue
on behalf of the world:
let blue be the color of the lake
while sleepers draw breaths
near the middle of the lawn

You really know the difference
the way pillows afford
a certain view of morning
Can you make a list
of the different kinds of roses?
To swim
to spell
to essentially
be led by the hand into
the same story
with a different
bear

*

One will speak of the median as if
it stabilized the argument as if
the time it takes light to travel
three times in two days
even flowers don't equal
themselves
their inner life
depending on the furniture
the delicate manifestation
of what makes papyrus
behave like papyrus

Life is eating
and entertaining
the desire to eat
something less familiar
like the wind and rain
prairie dogs make
in their prairie landscape
Are they selfsame
or is it like war in a less
familiar context?

*

Who is your leader
and how do you know?
the three cardinal flowers are five
the cardinals
bespoke
becoming a simple
exhibition of sense
in lieu of biscuits or
the blue of the blue edge
of the Pacific

Who thinks about apples
and who wants apples
for dinner
Whosoever considers
the leaves of the envelope open
to let the words out
standing on the edge
of the infinite pile
stumping
the pigeons

*

Life is a snowball moving faster
Her hands are not thinking
painted lilac
on the highway
to the bank of America
Can you aid the economy
by dropping
or rolling the yes
Say everything is related
Say it again
like the reflex
in the tulip
to alleviate doubt

Gumballs inhibit whispers
so disposed to idioms
of intellectual awakening
Maybe this is the only kind
of business casual I can handle
The movement of ideas
is panoramic
Yesterday for example
the skyscraper
embraced the sky
It really moves me
to believe in grass

*

It's hard to escape
the verbal equivalent
I was trying to apprehend
on her shirt
she said it gave me pause
it gave her
a thought experiment
I touched under her arm
or was it a thought itself
I pulled
from her book

Were they leaning into each other
as in dandelions leaning
about to say
You've forgotten
to think
the blue thought of leaves
will never yield
thickness
or hope
falling over whatever edge
you found in your ivy
deserter or denser

*

Pass your papers to the left
you do not
but we anticipated
and were allowed
to consider
the mute passenger
the vista from the copier
a wavy ribbon
the television left blinking
indecision like a face

Inclined, as it were,
to praying
by inventing diction
What you can see
in the greengrass
is sympathetic
a little wind
through which to pass
for example

*

Between window
and window washer
the point where lemon
meets the light
and in their makeshift
we plan for disaster
Now in the close-up
the birds float
A day is longer
in the arm
than rain

There is no finer example
of being useful if never
is a plum time
for no one
Who finally realized twice
to exit the sun
when actors
leave the stage for good
when she steps
on the beach
putting pressure
on the coast

*

So why is the lemon
more sufficient
in its equipment?
opening another hour
in the day
There is no vagabond
or lean-to
no X in the machinery to evolve
Now I face up to the living
and absorb savoir faire
while the poignant
nurse a pair in green ribbons

There must be
a more elegant approach
I am not horizontal
in the liquid
capturing the attitude
of enormous shadows
overlapping
poppies
If heat could talk
if hot were a color
it would not be red

*

Snow does understand
somewhere else
dark gold imprimatur
leaving the century
speaking of the valley
as a bowl
Maybe the car in its firmament
will purple
Maybe the genius
of her measure
will lift the daisy

If you have any doubts
the new
the familiar event
the sound of lovebirds
folding sweaters
in the eleventh century
Lovebirds are
to relativity
Sounds like trousers
walking forward in milk
forgetting to think

I Meant to Write You a Letter

It doesn't correspond
living in the sea

Nothing can survive here

It's the 19th century
again

Unlimited earth

That's what it means
to call home

The Other Part

i.

We're moving in alphabetical order

The red light is green behind

a small subtle wake that surrounds

the darkness and the time that spills

But let us suppose for a moment

if you heart that person

if you see her words move in the classical sense

when water is best

a finer atom like an element of love he said

I confess my wit, this sleepy edge

ii.

That's me getting it wrong

Everyone has motions they remove from the sky

supporting a house the lucky signs

a man who knows himself to be

bright or cloudy

In what troposphere are you whispering: light

in what place of thinking

We will keep his arms open in this poem

He is using his head again

he was here three times yesterday

Impossible Idiom

To think is to remember
lines sewn on a map
in equilateral stripes
(after Borges)
or dormant nature
in a teaspoon
(after Dickinson)
A synonym for self
is cyclorama
I am sorry
there is no hominid in this room
you can lean on
I like the way your trees behave
your use of earth
If you add more depth
if you divine
asleep in purple crush

The Poet Interrupts

I can't tell

a cat fight from a cloud

or quarters from saucers

and nonessential hums

that pierce every millimeter

in every least

visionary inch

searching for exits

in gamma forms

you can slip

into bureaucrats

choking on novelty

flapping like a soul

The Age of Parts

There were deeper colors
more flexible wool
I chorused beneath
I begged each zipper
in each Virginia
I said
I am sorry
No one smiles in a diver's throat
No one looks out from the inside
and asks, am I calling
Is this the place
a pilot beacons?
My good intentions rain
in buckets from a dome

*

The mind of this book
struggles to compose
One page provides an analogue
another provokes
a primary sense in green
and stolen bulbs
To interrupt our new arms
with movements
peace lovers
and little birds singing
in Greek
the business of this art cascades
it shows the influence of war
in a fig a perfect spark

*

I am ready to step toward
my material hand
I said to myself
moving slowly
like a lit hem along the end
About these you give a sign
or you decide
how you drive a wedge into
the industry of positive spoons
How being on fire is the same
living at the beginning
or the end
of the age of parts
We are not swimming

*

One day will be neon
I want to say with my hands
so you tell me
I put on my blue shirt
(emphasis yours)
and walk toward the fugue
If it is our purpose to remember
in these the dense arcs
the pools and black holes
we are not thinkers or islands that submit
when the sky quiets
when time machines
run out of gas

*

What is nonsense
and what is the afterlife
of a noisy thinker?
Some things lurch into being
and some things just happen
when nothing is left
but the courage
the relative frenzy
of what the navigator says
filling in the blanks
of a humble circumference
the courage of some
to live at the bottom
in a crevice

*

So adaptable is the mind
to the integrity of a grid
we inhabit a small parcel to fill
with elegant cubes
the morning
Lake water en route
to an underground beach
a dent
in thought
I don't know what I think you are:
Maybe the meaning of a common
window open
to a common street

*

This dovetails nicely
with freedom
or does it?
pushing a lark
out of the frame
in yellows of red
in reds of hermetic
complication
the little coins
the cold dandelions
of colder people
A tour de force on paper
A footnote to Ovid's
radiance

*

Add this to the atmosphere:
It's 5 a.m.
Experience happens
like lines
loving a hillside
If the first word on Wednesday
is railroad
or repair
How the avalanche moves
one envelope at a time
having driven or having had to drive
to get here
I am negative under the wind
because time is weird

*

Assuming the values
have their coordinates
we can home brew
appropriate vistas
for economic purposes
for all manner of
penultimate "scenes"
and "moments"
It was only a place to begin
and as with any "plan"
or "problem"
we were entangled
with the sun in public
watching ourselves
but not the whole panorama

*

One can take details from a still life
and render their motions
the hip of the glass
the body of the paint
one can see the difference
moving sideways
into pioneering research
or backward
from laundry
Thus it cannot be grasped
only absorbed by another
moving less than an inch per year
to record features
such as lying
and magic

*

Put an obelisk in the middle of history
and violently undermine
the tacit environment
of engineered stars
As one can take the desert
out of the ocean
and so produce intimations
of pivots and dents
Define: the sun's lonely
hummingbird
the moon's sinkhole
sinking
an aphorism about winter
between the knees

*

Becoming mineral
in an afternoon
the sun's pressure
an equivalent
to her blonde assassin
Among the miniature thoughts
in the garden
absorbing
life, I mean
How appealing are the pears
at home in the landscape
turning sunflowers
into avatars

*

Here is the hard kernel
of the whistle
the exit from the truth
like a big cloud
or a bigger bomb
Involutions of forgiveness
and waves evoked
by other waves
in the middle of nowhere
An ethics of loneliness
The massive lungs
of the people's
self-analysis
the inner lives
of circles and squares

*

How do you say?
the medium undergoes a metamorphosis
only for itself
The medium experiences
a derivation
Now we are different signs
me a paper bag and you
a floating barge
Me a clear space
and you
sun's silk
en route to de-wig
the future

*

Is there sense in a thought
when what gets lost
is heat, energy
Do you say
I saw the sun rise, or
the sun had risen over
the milky forest
taking shape
Do you ask
to what does the body belong
as manifold or failure
Under the covers or outside
in a question
There in a pivot between dirt
and a window

*

This proves I am not alone
walking the streets
trying to absorb
the scent of disaster
It never rhymes
When at the last moment
I was forgiven for
my life
I was forgiven on all accounts
when the telephone rang
I held on to my ideas
regarding the noisy rocks
and planets

*

The foreground also shakes
in the paragenetic song
abstract clouds drift over
the states
collecting nothing
No one floats above or loves
the dirt
Certain pedestals are full
of a poem's hand
and certain smaller bodies
in the ambit
of a lamp's arm
cracks

Queues

We have chosen to be
to live with effort
The water inside waits
As you can see
the matter is
where a blue span opens
The issue is sound
a pale clouded collector
parliament of arms

Something about Finches

I listen to corners where hands fumble

I am a thrush a piece of thread

It proves to be in other skirts

An *X* in the center laughing

An accent over what

A hum is not powerless to be

I am not the witness of

A swift secondary feature

Wind under a fire

This is only something I said I saw

Figurine

Take me to your gall
assay this airy paper
deep cuts
in an empty shell
Or should we say:
paper first
then dream later
A fine orb is a secret
in a single climber
bombardments
from the ether
ferocious dream cats
falling from earth
to apple

World Canary

Everywhere pink scrim acting like
everywhere earth conceals
the other is a heavy thought
a stitch that opens three times
giving what's at stake a push
into yellow hills if just
its tabletop and work that is
are ecothinking about crickets
to further one's need

The Age of Speculation

Drift is choice
This year ghosts meander

Something waits
inside love letters

something remembers
its many stones

In counterpanes you push against
what is useful in what is new

but what remains is either surprise
a patterned display

for example in the delicate
reader of trees who admits nothing

or a song in the middle
of its beginning

The actualities are drawn like bruises
the way genius will crash into lanterns

or simply windows
in numbered stripes on hillsides

Margaret Fuller

i.

I am that stranger
walking through

kitchen dust and pots
Please pledge your vivid

and your terse
your bold and nervous

humble acts and propositions
You may call me a woman

of modest steam in her time
I am printed matter

I am almost a sonnet
and hitherto defended

ii.

Whatever the eye swallows
is likely to rise up and come back:

the individual personal person
a green coat

familiar peculiar papers
characters emerging

from descriptions
pouring over

pictures of themselves
falling into edges

iii.

Here is a man who speaks on foot but fast asleep
the harness and handyman of whatnot
like a serious friend in a serious painting

Here are mouths that pull to the table a work
the *b* in bulb
an original thought
in pencil on paper
a sketch of lace in cahoots
in wheels
whistles

iv.

I am thinking about
what can change
and what becomes invisible
what is felt by itself
and what belongs to nervous feelings
and thrifty skirts
what moves forward into the future
and what stays behind in the hand
is not right now
not mountains and dominoes
or hills and sheets
What waits in a threshold
in wet hair

v.

It should be unmarvelous—
a language of open circles
and curled maps
of throaty coins that slip between
in thick knots

It should be historical
to undress a curtain
for the sake of understanding
ourselves and others
gathered midstream
but there is no grave and perfect being
neither the landscape nor the words
are significant

vi.

I touch a piece of this that isn't mine
in the room I did not invent

the age of two mouths
the age of what is meant by more

the age of wind
of cone and wire

A major figure is everyone here
a local heart

*

This song will convince no one
this dream hasn't begun

please fake a sense of decorum
on the way home

you won't believe how the energy escapes
the echo the arm

a torso collapses under the sigh
of a writer's minute

*

I am between trees
I would have said

my acts are bookish
and intense

my personal character sprawls
without instinct

my masculine impression of the dark
stems from failure

a tendency to float

vii.

Small early blooms
smaller than a shoestring
small enough to think or talk about
like sandals or summer
in another story

viii.

The hand that sang this song
was also once dramatic
a pilgrim moving into
another shape
stepping forward
in new shoes
taking its name from the discrete
middle arc
a particular detail
in a well-laid plan
a private shadow
asunder in a text

ix.

Whether festooned, battered,
or thrown backward
I am not the thread of my own subject
in the architect's
beachhead
I do not follow that path
nor use handrails
to greet the sun
I've been blown
sideways into buttons
blue and cold

x.

A common town listens to men
stepping over rocks

the wheels of a common town
push through

Let us not be mistaken
by a single wind

or the tissue inside shipwreck

Recall a stone a gladiola a something
holding light in a green cup

I could have spent my life thinking
in a window

I could have been a single
bird in a thumb

Complaint

The significance is wavy
You may call that an allegory of being

If you are not being undone
you are not living outside

as a public person
a public persona in a film

as a friend or a public
human being

becoming a seed
a new sound

a nickel on a hillside
five ways from Sunday

Green Is for World

for blowing seeds
for a rhyme I've sung to figs
long distance crossing sticks
for being in sync
in a car or over
for the temperature of the poem
tucked in her ears
will generate in the hand
for structures in leaves
getting thrown
off the page
being the first to think
you must be in possession
of a moment—
simple flowers for
simple prose

I can't remember
if I believe
an underground works
for water
a city waits
for days
stars are miniature habits
they do not recover
from disaster

I will not fight hard
but harder
for a writer's
handmade October
I've never done this before
holding accountable the air
craving details from the future
like lace or life in the arm

COLOPHON

Green Is for World was designed at Coffee House Press,
in the historic Grain Belt Brewery's Bottling House
near downtown Minneapolis.
Fonts include Garamond and Franklin Gothic Medium.

COFFEE HOUSE PRESS

MISSION

The mission of Coffee House Press is to publish exciting, vital, and enduring authors of our time; to delight and inspire readers; to contribute to the cultural life of our community; and to enrich our literary heritage. By building on the best traditions of publishing and the book arts, we produce books that celebrate imagination, innovation in the craft of writing, and the many authentic voices of the American experience.

VISION

LITERATURE. We will promote literature as a vital art form, helping to redefine its role in contemporary life. We will publish authors whose groundbreaking work helps shape the direction of 21st-century literature. **WRITERS.** We will foster the careers of our writers by making long-term commitments to their work, allowing them to take risks in form and content. **READERS.** Readers of books we publish will experience new perspectives and an expanding intellectual landscape. **PUBLISHING.** We will be leaders in developing a sustainable 21st-century model of independent literary publishing, pushing the boundaries of content, form, editing, audience development, and book technologies.

VALUES

Innovation and excellence in all activities
Diversity of people, ideas, and products
Advancing literary knowledge
Community through embracing many cultures
Ethical and highly professional management and governance practices

Good books are brewing at coffeehousepress.org

FUNDER ACKNOWLEDGMENT

Coffee House Press is an independent, nonprofit literary publisher. Our books are made possible through the generous support of grants and gifts from many foundations, corporate giving programs, state and federal support, and through donations from individuals who believe in the transformational power of literature. Coffee House Press receives major operating support from the Bush Foundation, the Jerome Foundation, the McKnight Foundation, the National Endowment for the Arts—a federal agency, from Target, and in part, from the Minnesota State Arts Board through the arts and cultural heritage fund as appropriated by the Minnesota State Legislature with money from the Legacy Amendment vote of the people of Minnesota on November 4, 2008. Coffee House also receives support from: several anonymous donors; Suzanne Allen; Elmer L. and Eleanor J. Andersen Foundation; Around Town Agency; Patricia Beithon; Bill Berkson; the E. Thomas Binger and Rebecca Rand Fund of the Minneapolis Foundation; the Patrick and Aimee Butler Family Foundation; Ruth Dayton; Dorsey & Whitney, LLP; Mary Ebert and Paul Stembler; Chris Fischbach and Katie Dublinski; Fredrikson & Byron, P.A.; Sally French; Anselm Hollo and Jane Dalrymple-Hollo; Jeffrey Hom; Carl and Heidi Horsch; Alex and Ada Katz; Stephen and Isabel Keating; the Kenneth Koch Literary Estate; Kathy and Dean Koutsky; the Lenfestey Family Foundation; Carol and Aaron Mack; Mary McDermid; Sjur Midness and Briar Andresen; the Rehael Fund of the Minneapolis Foundation; Schwegman, Lundberg & Woessner, P.A.; Kiki Smith; Jeffrey Sugerman; Patricia Tilton; the Archie D. & Bertha H. Walker Foundation; Stu Wilson and Mel Barker; the Woessner Freeman Family Foundation; Margaret and Angus Wurtele; and many other generous individual donors.

ART WORKS.

MINNESOTA
STATE ARTS BOARD

TARGET.

To you and our many readers across the country,
we send our thanks for your continuing support.

THE NATIONAL POETRY SERIES

Coffee House Press is proud to be a participating publisher in the National Poetry Series. For more information, please visit their website at nationalpoetryseries.org.

Sarah—Of Fragments and Lines by Julie Carr (2011)
In the wake of a mother's battle with Alzheimer's and a child's impending birth, Carr gathers the shards of mourning and joy to give voice to the longing that accompanies life's most profound losses and its most anticipated arrivals.

Exhibit of Forking Paths by James Grinwis (2010)
These poems pair electrical circuit diagrams with prose poems to create an artful labyrinth of science, intellectual landscapes, and urban scenes. The title of the collection comes from a story by Jorge Luis Borges, "Garden of Forking Paths."

Catch Light by Sarah O'Brien (2009)
In *Catch Light,* photography—its history, its technology, and the ways it captures and changes the world—meets poetry, locating reality in illusion and throwing open the windows of visual narrative. "The whole / world is synonyms."

The Cosmopolitan by Donna Stonecipher (2007)
These poems travel a world both romantic and politicized, miniaturized by globalization and haunted by the cosmopolitan, who, aware of its saturated history, is inspired by the knowledge that nostalgia is merely "memory decayed to sugar."

Teahouse of the Almighty by Patricia Smith (2006)
"Searing, honest, well-crafted, and full of the real world transformed by Smith's fine ear for nuance and the shaking of the soul's duties. I was weeping for the beauty of poetry when I reached the end."
—EDWARD SANDERS, JUDGE

Starred Wire by Ange Mlinko (2004)
Hailed by *Publishers Weekly* as "one of the most exciting American poets under 40," Mlinko's *Starred Wire* reaches across continents of language, where dream logic dictates a delirious exploration of art and childhood, place and possibility.

Murder (a violet) by Raymond McDaniel (2003)
"Action, violent and noir, alternates with passages reminiscent of Japanese landscape scrolls—all composed, with a light touch and an ear sensitive to the weights and balances of words, into a poem that rewards rereading." —ANSELM HOLLO, JUDGE

That Kind of Sleep by Susan Atefat Peckham (2000)
Behind the curtain that has historically concealed the lives of Iranian women, images whet and sting the senses—rich fabrics, earthy scents—and her celebration of family and culture burnish this collection to a touching glow.

Madame Deluxe by Tenaya Darlington (1999)
Madame Deluxe is all things loud and leopard print. Darlington evokes a persona who wanders the periphery, catcalling Venus and Victoria's Secret—a she-male Vesuvius. Seductive and shocking, these poems rethink "woman" and "femininity."

Good books are brewing at coffeehousepress.org